MULTIDISCIPLINARY
SPACES

·····················

architectural complexes

monsa

MULTIDISCIPLINARY SPACES
Copyright © 2016 Instituto Monsa de ediciones

Editor, concept, and project director
Josep María Minguet

Project's selection, design and layout
Patricia Martínez (equipo editorial Monsa)

INSTITUTO MONSA DE EDICIONES
Gravina 43 (08930)
Sant Ádria de Besòs
Barcelona (Spain)
Tlf. +34 93 381 00 50
www.monsa.com
monsa@monsa.com

Visit our official online store!
www.monsashop.com

Follow us on facebook!
facebook.com/monsashop

ISBN: 978-84-16500-07-9
D.L. B 26817-2015
Printed by Cachimán Grafic

Introduction

What is Multidisciplinary Architecture? We see it as a type of architecture which is able to create a stimulating effect through spatial organisation.

A Multidisciplinary building is generally used by the general public, and one that includes large multi-purpose spaces. Each activity area leads into a hall, which acts as a common link between them, thus creating a dynamic area where information, relations, leisure and culture are intermingled and mutually enhanced.

Some multidisciplinary buildings are cultural centres which include an auditorium, a theatre, rehearsal area, events room...others are sports facilities which contain different pitches and courts, for basketball, indoor football, etc. combined with educational areas such as libraries, and areas set aside for workshops. A good example is the Zamet Centre, which provides not only sports facilities but also a library, shops and service areas. Another building which stands out is the MUCAB architectural complex, which consists of a museum, a music school, a local development centre, a child service centre and nursery school.

The book includes a range of interesting architectural projects of this kind: spaces with an innovative design and their own personality which are not only interesting and important *per se*, in view of everything they represent, but which also help to promote the cities where they are located, because they become flagship buildings which draw people's interest.

Entendemos la Arquitectura Multidisciplinar, como aquella que consigue crear un efecto estimulador, a través de la organización espacial.

El edificio multidisciplinar es normalmente de uso público y en él se integran grandes espacios de usos múltiples, cada área de actividades se vincula a un vestíbulo, que actúa como nexo de unión entre todas, consiguiendo un espacio dinámico en el que la información, relación, el ocio y la cultura se encuentran, enriqueciéndose entre sí.

Algunos de ellos son centros culturales que incluyen un auditorio, un teatro, sala de ensayos, sala de eventos... otros son edificios de instalaciones deportivas en los que encontraremos diferentes pistas, de básquet, de fútbol sala, etc. combinadas con zonas lúdicas como bibliotecas, y áreas para talleres. En este sentido encontramos ejemplos como el Centro Zamet, que además de instalaciones deportivas incluye una biblioteca, comercios y zonas de servicio. Otro edificio destacable es el conjunto arquitectónico MUCAB, compuesto por un museo, una escuela de música, un centro de desarrollo local, un centro de atención a la infancia y una guardería.

El libro incluye una selección de diversos e interesantes proyectos de este tipo de arquitectura; espacios con un diseño innovador y personalidad propia que no solo son interesantes e importantes por todo lo que engloban si no que a su vez ayudan a promocionar las ciudades donde se ubican, convirtiéndose en puntos de referencia y de interés.

Palace of International Forums Uzbekistan

Tashkent, Uzbekistan

ARCHITECT:
Ippolito Fleitz Group
www.ifgroup.org

DIMENSIONS:
40,000 m² / 430,570 sq ft

PHOTOGRAPHERS:
© Zooey Braun, Andreas J. Focke

COLLABORATORS AND OTHERS:
Peter Ippolito, Gunter Fleitz, Steffen Ringler,
Tilla Goldberg, Silke Schreier, Swetlana Wagner,
Christine Ackermann, Alexander Fehre,
Christian Kirschenmann, Tim Lessmann,
Jakub Pakula, Hakan Sakarya, Jörg Schmitt,
Mortiz Köhler, Daniela Schröder, Julia Weigle,
Frank Fassmer, Axel Knapp, Yuan Peng,
Michael Bertram, Elena Nuthmann-Maysyuk,
Klaus-Dieter Nuthmann (team)

The building was designed to accommodate acts of state, congresses, conferences and cultural events. The architects' main task was to give a contemporary form to the interior, which will incorporate elements of the traditional Uzbek architecture. The exterior combines classical elements with a modern glass façade.

El edificio se concibió para acoger los actos de Estado, congresos, conferencias y eventos culturales. La principal tarea de los arquitectos consistió en dotar al interior de una forma contemporánea que incorporara elementos de la arquitectura tradicional uzbeka. El exterior combina elementos clásicos con una fachada moderna acristalada.

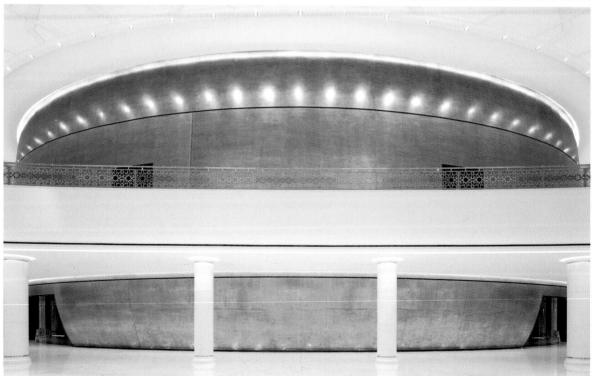

The building's interior is cosmopolitan and communicative, dressed with exclusive materials, crystals, precious metals and interactions of natural and artificial light.

El interior del edificio resulta cosmopolita y comunicativo, vestido con materiales exclusivos, cristales, metales preciosos y una interacción de luz artificial y natural.

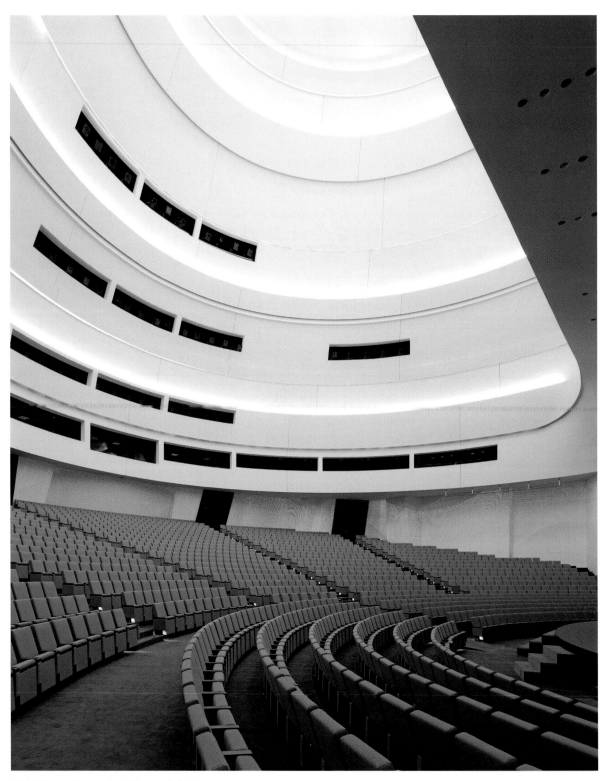

Belfry Tashkent

Tashkent, Uzbekistan

ARCHITECT:
Ippolito Fleitz Group
www.ifgroup.org

DIMENSIONS:
340 m² / 3,659.8 sq ft

PHOTOGRAPHER:
© Zooey Braun

COLLABORATORS AND OTHERS:
Peter Ippolito, Gunter Fleitz, Tilla Goldberg,
Steffen Ringler, Alexander Fehre,
Christian Kirschenmann (team); RIEDL Messebau,
Landenbau und Objektbau (general contractor);
Pfarré lighting design (lighting)

The jewelry shop forms part of the Uzbekistan International Forums Palace, inaugurated in 2009 in order to celebrate the 2200 anniversary of the city of Tashkent. The original design is like entering into the interior of an adorned jewelry box. The rooms are designed to translate the exhibitions' products' character of exclusivity.

La tienda de joyas forma parte del Palacio Uzbekistan International Forums, inaugurado en el 2009 para celebrar el 2200 aniversario de la ciudad de Tashkent. El diseño original es como entrar en el interior de una caja de joyería adornada. Las salas están pensadas para transmitir el carácter de exclusividad de los productos en exhibición.

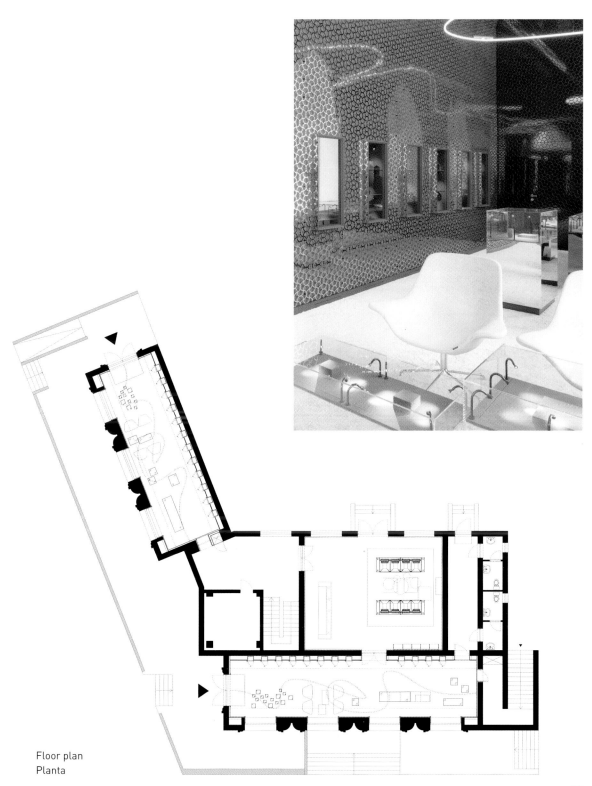

Floor plan
Planta

Miguel Delibes Cultural Center

Valladolid, Spain

ARCHITECT:
Ricardo Bofill Taller de Arquitectura
www.bofill.com

DIMENSIONS:
40,000 m² / 430,570.5 sq ft

COLLABORATORS AND OTHERS:
UTE Auditorio Zarzuela, Dragados (builders)

PHOTOGRAPHER:
© Carlos Casariego

The architectural combination is a great translucent space inside of which some boxes are situated (experimental theatre, auditorium and bedroom halls), with their pertinent schools (music conservatory, schools of theater and dance school). The complex is a new meeting place and cultural exchange for the whole city.

El conjunto arquitectónico es un gran espacio diáfano en cuyo interior se ubican unas cajas (sala de cámara, auditorio y teatro experimental), junto con sus escuelas pertinentes (conservatorio de música, escuelas de teatro y escuela de danza). El complejo es un nuevo lugar de encuentro e intercambio cultural para la ciudad.

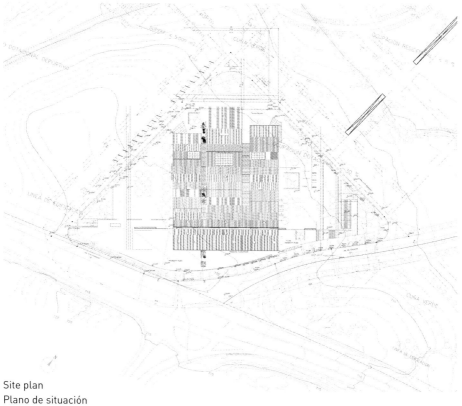

Site plan
Plano de situación

Ground floor plan
Planta baja

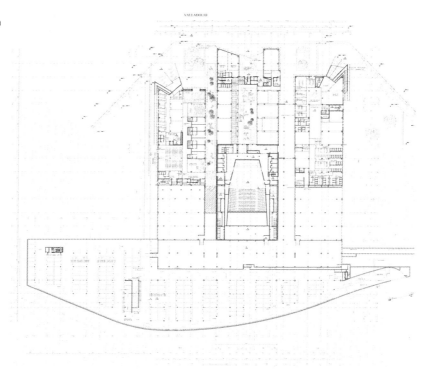

First floor plan
Planta primera

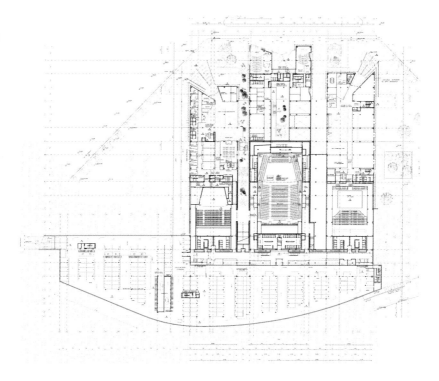

The covered square that joins the different sectors is conceived as an interactive atrium that allows the students to interact amongst themselves and with the professionals and the public.

La plaza cubierta que une los diferentes sectores se concibe como un atrio interactivo que permite a los estudiantes relacionarse entre ellos y con los profesionales y el público.

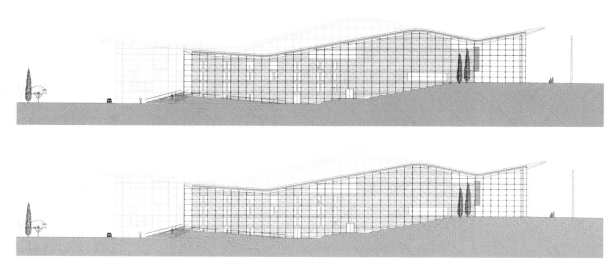

Elevations
Alzados

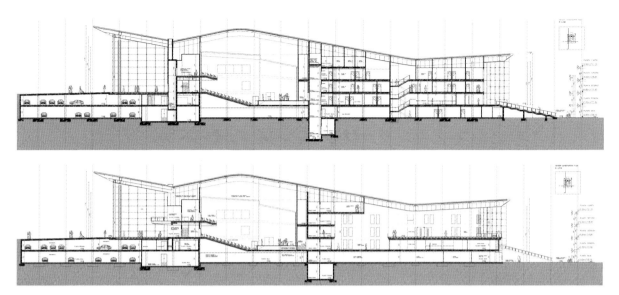

Sections
Secciones

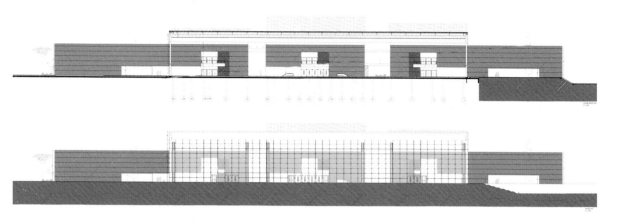

South elevation and section
Alzado sur y sección

LanQiao clubhouse

Rizhao, China

ARCHITECT:
HHD_FUN
www.hhdfun.com

DIMENSIONS:
1,150 m² / 12,378.9 sq ft

COLLABORATORS AND OTHERS:
XinChao Design (team); H&J International
(civil engineer); FUDA (façade consultant)

PHOTOGRAPHERS:
© Zhenfei Wang, Chenggui Wang

The building is located in the southern part of the Shanhaitian park and includes saunas, cafes and a swimming pool. Each installation is unique, so that the set offers a full tourist experience to visitors. The building was built towards the sea to preserve the forest and its form is minimized to fit into the natural environment.

El edificio se sitúa en la parte sur del parque Shanhaitian e incluye saunas, cafés y una piscina. Cada instalación es única, de manera que el conjunto ofrece una completa experiencia turística a los visitantes. Para preservar el bosque, el edificio fue construido hacia el mar, y su forma se minimiza para encajar en el entorno natural.

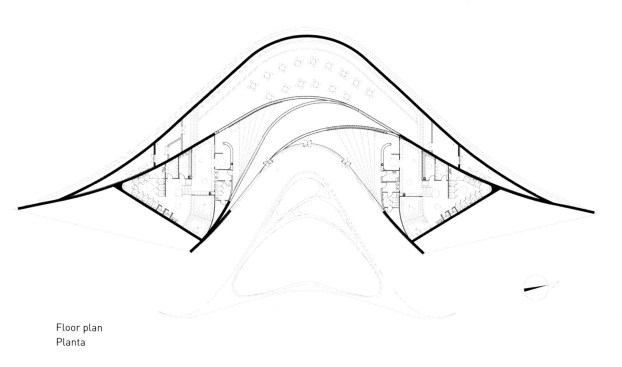

Floor plan
Planta

The parametric design technique has been used throughout the design process. The steel structure is adapted to support the complex construction.

La técnica del diseño paramétrico se ha utilizado a lo largo de todo el proceso de diseño. La estructura de acero es el soporte adaptado a la compleja construcción.

Myrtus Conventions Centre

Puçol, Spain

ARCHITECT:
Ramón Esteve Estudio
www.ramonesteve.com

DIMENSIONS:
5,712.06 m² / 61,486.1 sq ft

PHOTOGRAPHERS:
© Eugeni Pons, Léa Chave,
Sergio Pomar

COLLABORATORS AND OTHERS:
Olga Badía, María Daroz, Daniela Adame,
Silvia M. Martínez, Emilio Pérez (team);
Construcciones Francés (builder)

The project's proposal is to generate a building that serves to accommodate large events, with capacity for up to a thousand people. The organic geometry of the building, developed in a circular theme, produces continuous and fluid spaces, which stimulate free movement in a flexible space. The sinuous line confers a friendly character to the building.

El planteamiento del proyecto es generar un edificio que sirva para acoger grandes eventos, con capacidad para hasta mil personas. La geometría orgánica del edificio, desarrollada sobre una trama circular, genera espacios continuos y fluidos, que inducen a moverse libremente en un espacio flexible. La línea sinuosa confiere al edificio un carácter amable.

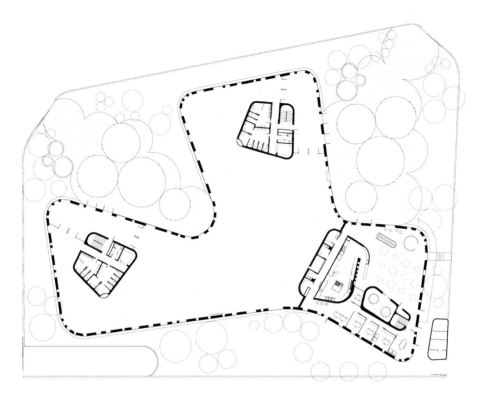

Floor plan
Planta

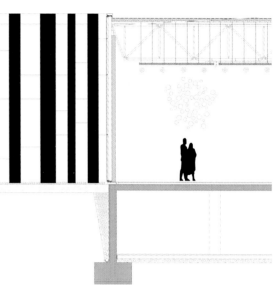

Enlarged detailed section
Sección detallada ampliada

Section facing west
Sección orientación oeste

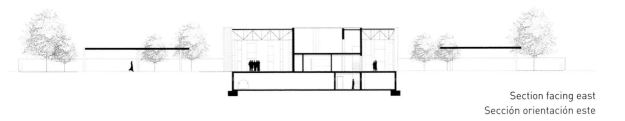

Section facing east
Sección orientación este

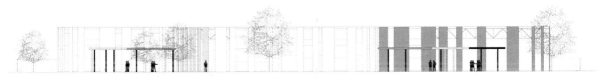

East elevation
Alzado este

West elevation
Alzado oeste

The programme consists in 3 floors: the ground floor accommodates the conference halls; the offices and the restaurant are on the first floor; and the parking is in the basement.

El programa consiste en 3 plantas: la planta baja alberga los salones de convenciones; en la primera planta están las oficinas y el restaurante; y en el sótano, el aparcamiento.

Platoon Kunsthalle

Seoul, Korea / Berlin, Germany

ARCHITECT:
GRAFT-Gesellschaft von Architekten
www.graftlab.com

DIMENSIONS:
Seoul 415 m^2; Berlin 435 m^2 /
Seoul 4,467.1 sq ft; Berlin 4,682.4 sq ft

PHOTOGRAPHER:
© Courtesy of Platoon and Platoon Kunsthalle Berlin

These are two mobile buildings that consist of between 28 and 34 cargo containers each accommodating spaces in which to perform symposia, workshops, conferences and events. The containers are installed stacked to form a unique construction that can be rebuilt in any other place.

Se trata de dos edificios móviles que constan de entre 28 y 34 contenedores de carga cada uno, para albergar espacios en los que hacer simposios, talleres, conferencias y eventos. Los contenedores se instalan de manera apilada para formar una construcción única que puede reconstruirse en cualquier otro lugar.

These containers are icons of a flexible architecture in a globalized culture. The interior has also been developed by Platoon.

Estos contenedores son iconos de una arquitectura flexible en una cultura globalizada. El interior también ha sido desarrollado por Platoon.

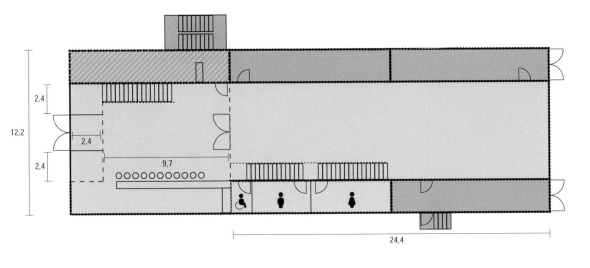

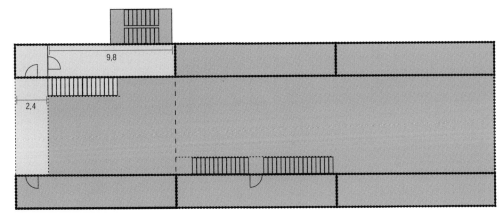

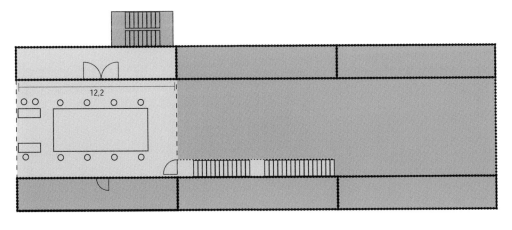

Floor plans
Plantas

Tlaxcala State Office Public Education and Health

Tlaxcala, Mexico

ARCHITECT:
JS^a
www.jsa.com.mx

DIMENSIONS:
46,420 m² / 499,677 sq ft

PHOTOGRAPHER:
© Paul Rivera

COLLABORATORS AND OTHERS:
Javier Sánchez, Juan Manuel Soler,
Aisha Ballesteros, Milton Duran, Gabriela Delgado,
DMG Arquitectos (team); Miguel de la Torre,
Cesar Brito, Zulkerine Cazares (executive project);
Hector Margain y Asociados (engineer)

Offices of two ministries at the Tlaxcala state, public education and health, are located in the middle of an urban context where residences prevail. Because these buildings designed as staggered terraces had to be built quickly, a structural system based on prefabricated material was opted for.

Las oficinas de dos ministerios del Estado de Tlaxcala, el de Educación Pública y el de Salud, se sitúan en medio de un contexto urbano en el que predominan las residencias. Dado que estos edificios, pensados como terrazas escalonadas, tuvieron que ser construidos rápidamente, se optó por un sistema estructural basado en el material prefabricado.

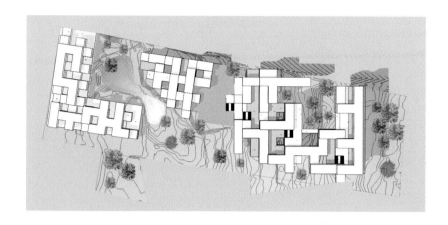

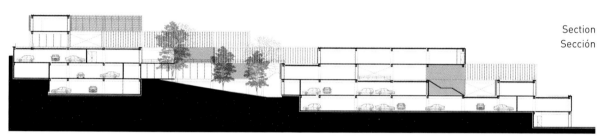

Section
Sección

Reconversion of Mies van der Rohe gas station

Verdun, Canada

ARCHITECT:
Les Architectes FABG
www.arch-fabg.com

DIMENSIONS:
N/A

PHOTOGRAPHER:
© Steve Montpetit

COLLABORATORS AND OTHERS:
Éric Gauthier (principal architect); Marc Paradis,
Dominique Potvin, Jaime Lopez,
Steve Montpetit (team); Aecom (engineer);
Norgéreq (builder)

This prototype designed by Mies Van Der Rohe in 1966 has been set up in an open space for recreational activities. The building is composed of two different volumes, which have been restored without affecting the heritage value of whoever enjoys the construction. The black building is intended for adolescents and the white building for young people.

Este prototipo diseñado por Mies van der Rohe en 1966 se ha habilitado en un espacio abierto para albergar actividades lúdicas. El edificio se compone de dos volúmenes distintos, que han sido restaurados sin afectar al valor patrimonial del que goza la construcción. El edificio negro está destinado a los adolescentes y el blanco, a los jóvenes.

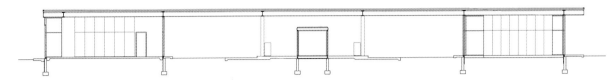

Section
Sección

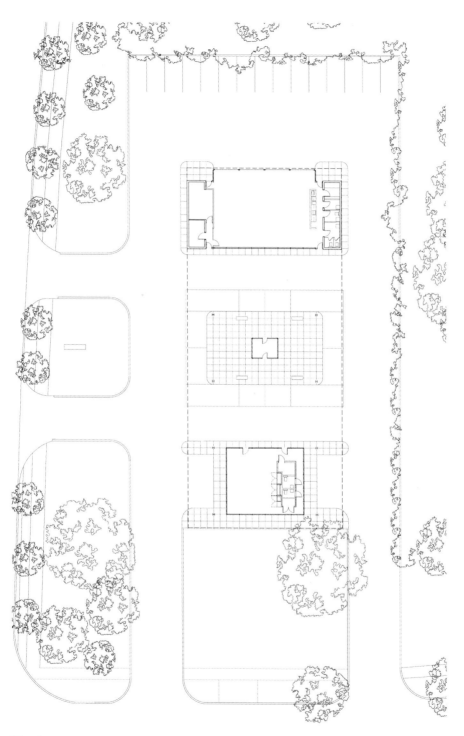

Site plan
Plano de situación

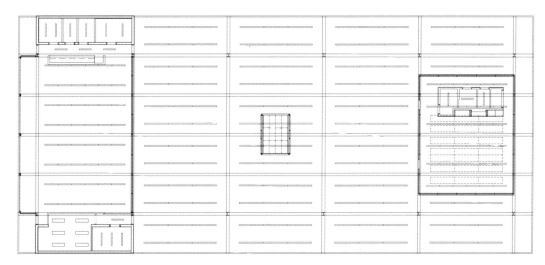

Reflected ceiling plan
Plano del techo reflejado

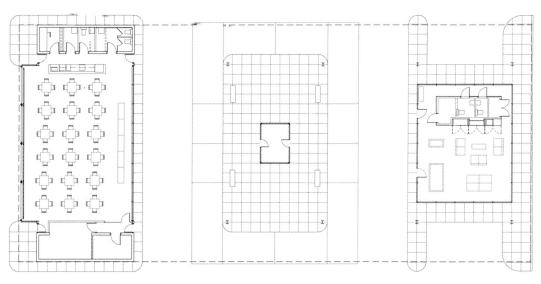

Floor plan
Planta

Claire and Marc Bourgie Pavilion

Montreal, Canada

ARCHITECT:
Provencher Roy + Associés Architectes
www.praa.qc.ca

DIMENSIONS:
5,483 m² / 59,020.45 sq ft

PHOTOGRAPHERS:
© Tom Arban, Alexi Hobbs, Marc
Cramer, Jean-Guy Lambert

COLLABORATORS AND OTHERS:
Claude Provencher, Mattieu Geoggrion, Eugenio
Carelli, Jean-Luc Rémy,
Denis Gamache (team); Gesvel (project
management); Pomerlau (general contractor and
construction management)

The project consists in the conversion of a church into an art pavilion. The rear annex has been completely rebuilt in a contemporary style to form the new pavilion next to the old and restored church, transformed into a concert hall with capacity for 444 persons. The new art pavilion provides a natural dialogue with the city. The openings of the glass atrium offer a view of the city and Mount Royal.

El proyecto consiste en la conversión de una iglesia en un pabellón de arte. Junto a la antigua y restaurada iglesia, transformada en una sala de conciertos con capacidad para 444 personas, el anexo trasero ha sido completamente reconstruido en un estilo contemporáneo para formar el pabellón nuevo. El nuevo pabellón de arte establece un diálogo natural con la ciudad. Las aberturas del atrio acristalado ofrecen una vista de la ciudad y del Mount Royal.

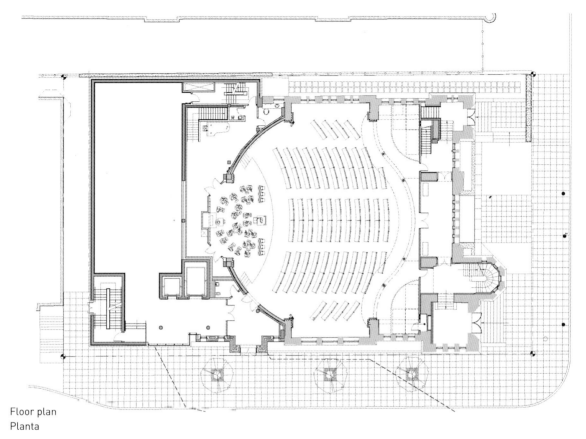

Floor plan
Planta

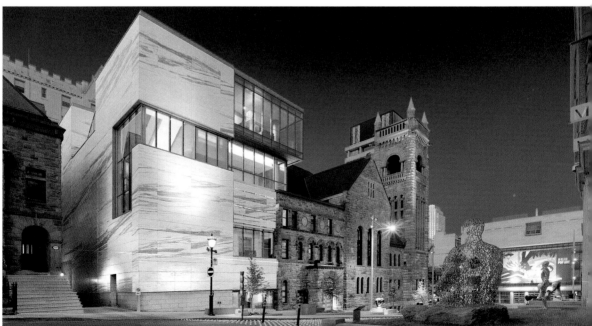

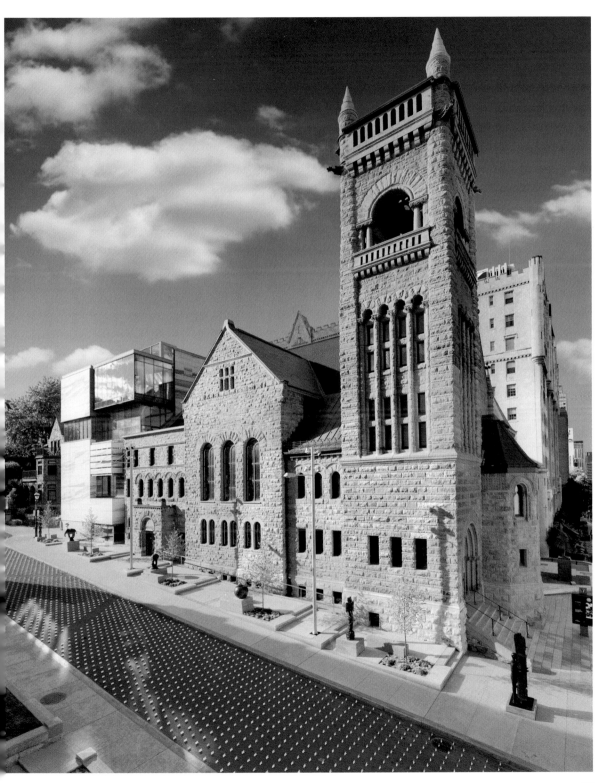

MUCAB

Murcia, Spain

ARCHITECT:
Martín Lejarraga
www.lejarraga.com

DIMENSIONS:
2,150 m² / 23,143.1 sq ft

PHOTOGRAPHER:
© David Frutos

COLLABORATORS AND OTHERS:
Juan García Carrillo, Francisco Pérez,
Manuel Gil de Pareja, Mar Melgarejo,
Arancha Fernández, Julián Lloret (team);
Villegas (builder)

The architectural complex is composed by a museum (central area); a music school; a center for local development, women and youth (north building); a crèche, and a center for child care (ground floor). The building is grouped into three programmatic packages connected by courtyards, but each one works in an independent way.

El conjunto arquitectónico se compone de un museo (espacio central); una escuela de música; un centro de desarrollo local, de la mujer y de la juventud (edificio norte); una guardería, y un centro de atención a la infancia (planta baja). El edificio se agrupa en tres paquetes programáticos conectados por patios, pero cada uno funciona de manera independiente.

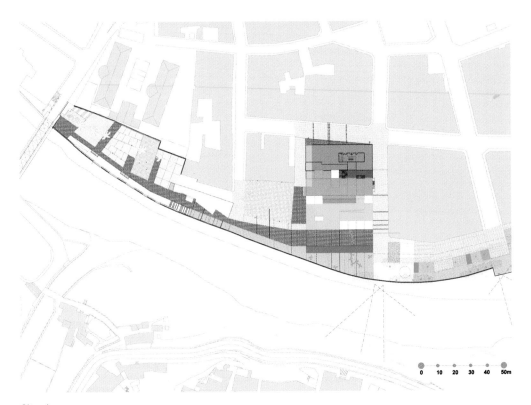

Site plan
Plano de situación

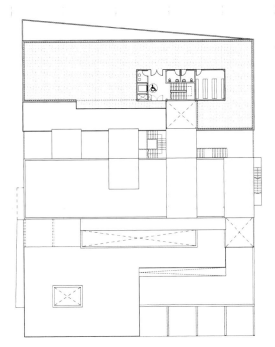

Roof plan
Planta de la cubierta

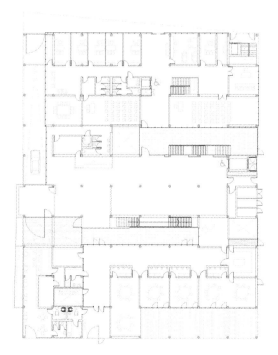

Ground floor plan
Planta baja

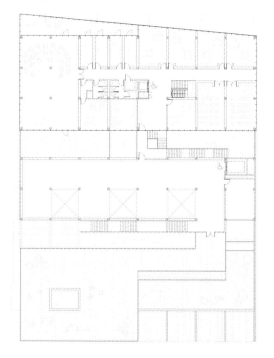

First floor plan
Planta primera

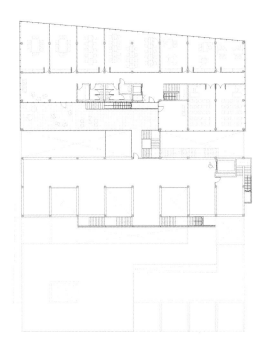

Second floor plan
Planta segunda

Third floor plan
Planta tercera

Upper courtyards let natural light in by perforating their cover and permit ventilation and visual connection with other uses of the building.

Los patios superiores perforan su cubierta de modo que introducen luz natural y permiten la ventilación y la conexión visual con el resto de usos del edificio.

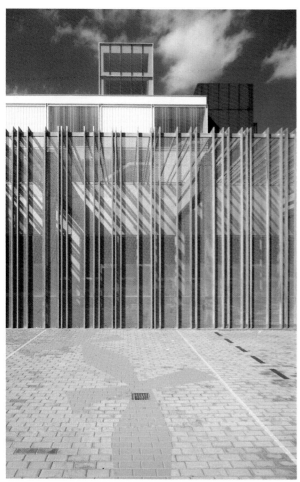

Zamet Center

Zamet, Croatia

ARCHITECT:
3LHD Architects
www.3lhd.com

DIMENSIONS:
16,830 m² / 181,162.5 sq ft

PHOTOGRAPHERS:
© Domagoj Blažević, Damir Fabijanić,
3LHD archive

COLLABORATORS AND OTHERS:
Saša Begović, Tatjana Grozdanić Begović,
Marko Drabović, Silvije Novak, Paula Kukuljica,
Zvonimir Marčić, Leon Lazanero, Eugen Popović,
Nives Krsnik, Andrea Vukojić (team);
GP Krk (main contractor)

The Zamet sports complex hosts diverse sports facilities with capacity for 2,380 persons, offices, a library, shops, services and a parking area. The main architectural element of the building are the horizontal stripes that extend in a north-south direction; they function as a decorative element and area separator.

El complejo deportivo Zamet alberga diversas instalaciones deportivas con capacidad para 2.380 personas, oficinas, una biblioteca, comercios, servicios y una zona de aparcamiento. El principal elemento arquitectónico del edificio son las franjas horizontales que se extienden en dirección norte-sur; funcionan como elemento decorativo y separador de zonas.

To create the stripes in the form of ribbons they were inspired by gromača, a specific type of Rijeka rock that reinterprets the color and shape of the center artificially.

Para crear las franjas en forma de cintas se inspiraron en gromača, un tipo de rocas específicas de Rijeka que reinterpreta el centro de manera artificial por el color y la forma.

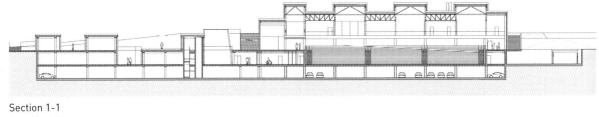

Section 1-1
Sección 1-1

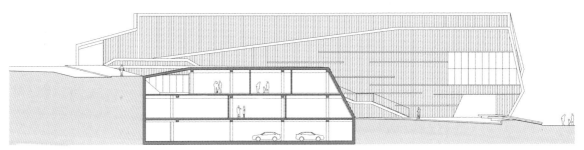

Section A-A
Sección A-A

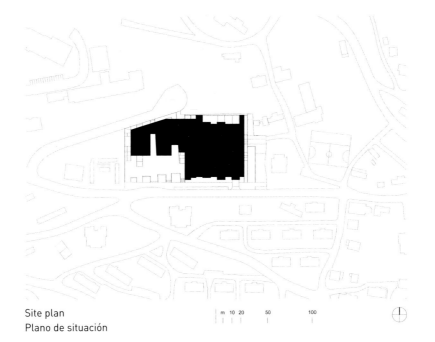

Section B-B
Sección B-B

Site plan
Plano de situación

m 10 20   50   100

Roof plan
Planta de la cubierta

m   10   20   50

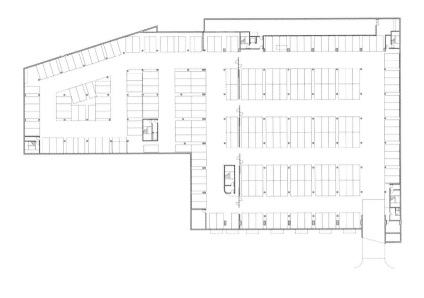

Basement floor
Planta sótano

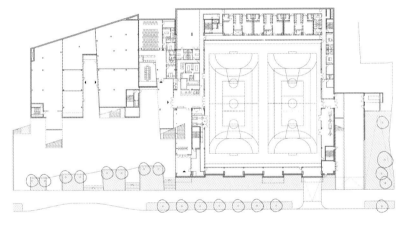

Ground floor plan
Planta baja

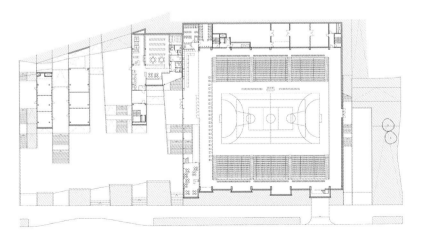

First floor plan
Planta primera

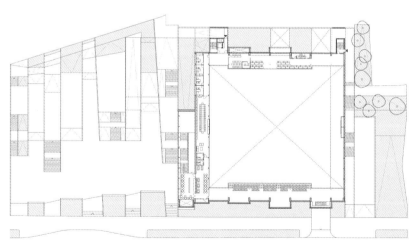

Second floor plan
Planta segunda

Nebuta-no-ie Warasse

Aomori, Japan

ARCHITECT:
Molo; d & dt Arch;
Frank la Rivière Architects
www.molodesign.com
www.d-dt.co.jp
www.frank-la-riviere.com

DIMENSIONS:
4,339 m² / 46,706.1 sq ft

PHOTOGRAPHERS:
© Frank la Rivière, Shigeo Ogawa

COLLABORATORS AND OTHERS:
Kanebako Structural Engineers (structure);
PT Morimura & Associates (MEP);
Kajima, Fukimoto, Kurahashi
Construction JV (builder)

This construction revolves around the Nebuta festival. The aspect of the building that stands out most is the 12 metre high screen with steel belts that envelops the whole construction and closes in an open air walkway. Each belt is twisted and folded to form openings in which the lighting, the viewpoints and walkways are situated.

Esta construcción gira en torno al festival de Nebuta. El aspecto más destacado del edificio es la pantalla de doce metros de altura con cintas de acero que envuelve toda la construcción y encierra un paseo al aire libre. Cada cinta se tuerce y se dobla para formar aberturas en las que se sitúan la iluminación, los miradores y las pasarelas.

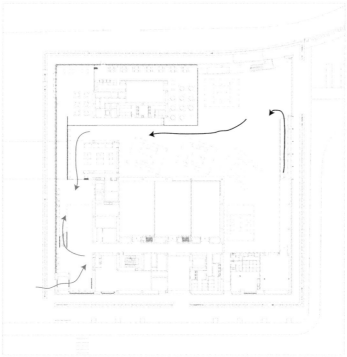

First floor plan
Planta primera

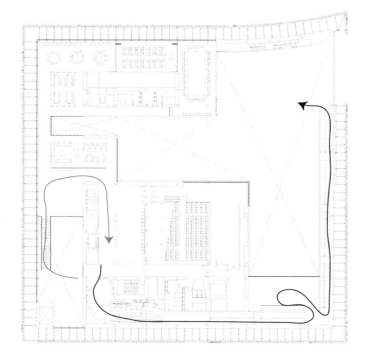

Second floor plan
Planta segunda

—— main route visitors (free area)
—— **main route visitors (paid area)**

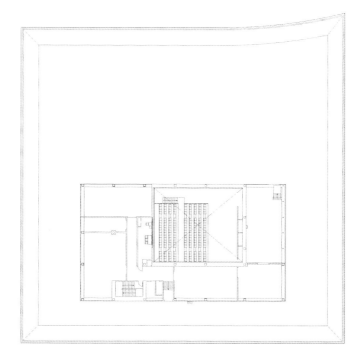

Third floor plan
Planta tercera

Exhibition spaces presenting the history of the Nebuta festival and of the city of Aomori, a restaurant and multi-purpose rooms are found in the interior.

En el interior se ubican salas de exposición sobre la historia del festival de Nebuta y la ciudad de Aomori, un restaurante y espacios de usos múltiples.

The Shanxi Grand Theater

Taiyuan, China

ARCHITECT:
Arte Charpentier Architectes
www.arte-charpentier.com

DIMENSIONS:
73,000 m² / 785,791.1 sq ft

PHOTOGRAPHER:
© Shen Zhonghai

COLLABORATORS AND OTHERS:
Sun Hongliang, Antonio Frausto, Lai Xiangbin,
Song Yang, Feng Yiqin, Cai Zhaiyu (team);
Shanxi Architectural Institute, Jacques Moyal
(main consultants); Shanxi Building General
Company (contractor)

The building is designed as an urban sculpture, and its façade is characterized by a grainy texture that plays with the light. Inside, 1,600 seating room is located to the north and two small rooms to the south. The building which is emblematic for the city and its inhabitants, has become an element of social and urban identity.

El edificio está diseñado como una escultura urbana, y su fachada se caracteriza por una piel de granito que juega con la luz. En el interior se ubica una sala de 1.600 asientos en la parte norte y dos salas más pequeñas al sur. El edificio, emblemático para la ciudad y sus habitantes, se ha convertido en un elemento de la identidad social y urbana.

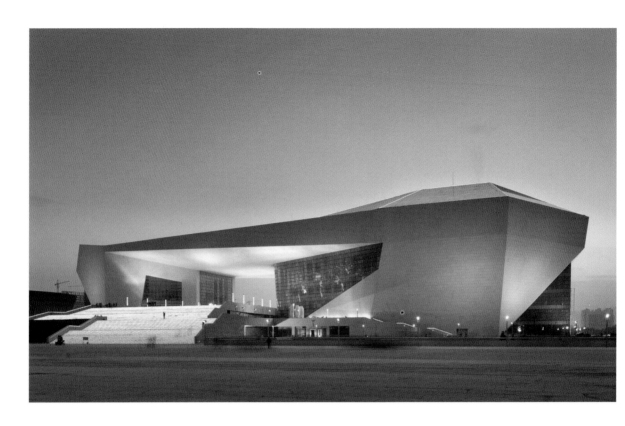

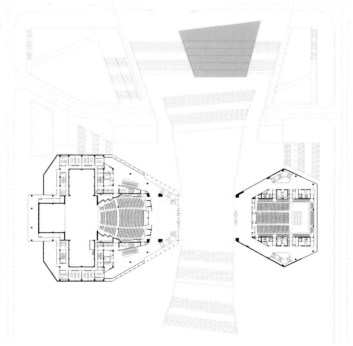

Plans
Planos

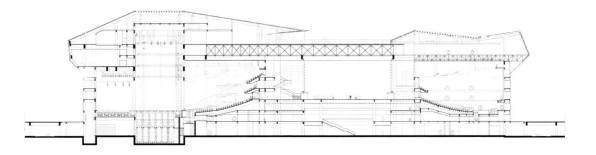

Sections
Secciones

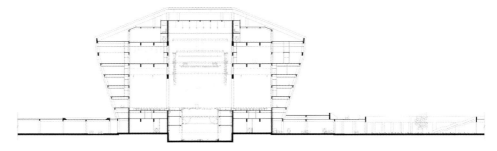

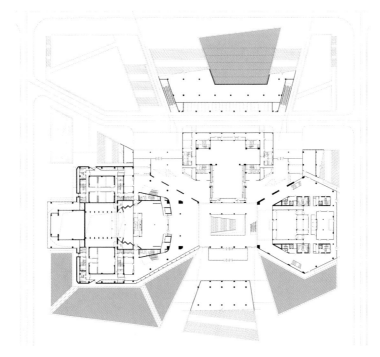

Plans
Planos

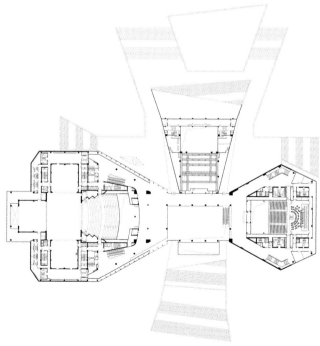

Plans
Planos

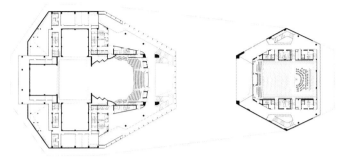

Plans
Planos

Parque de Lectura

Torre Pacheco, Spain

ARCHITECT:
Martín Lejarraga
www.lejarraga.com

DIMENSIONS:
84,000 m² / 904,198 sq ft

PHOTOGRAPHER:
© David Frutos

COLLABORATORS AND OTHERS:
Mar Melgarejo, Claudia Montoya, Ana López,
Daniel Ruiz Zurita, Ana Martínez, Javier Poeda,
Teresa Talaya (team); Ferrovial-Agromán (builder);
ACE Edificación, Mariano Alegría, José Ibeas,
Pedro Ruiz (consultants)

The Project appears beginning from a new planning in one of the city's extension areas. This plot consists of public equipment for the citizens' enjoyment. The open air park stands out, that enjoys special conditions of the Mediterranean climate and social life for the interaction of different ethnicities.

El proyecto aparece a partir de una nueva ordenación en una zona de extensión de la ciudad. Esta parcela consta de equipamientos públicos para el disfrute de los ciudadanos. Destaca el parque al aire libre, que aprovecha las especiales condiciones del clima mediterráneo, y la vida social de la interrelación de diferentes etnias.

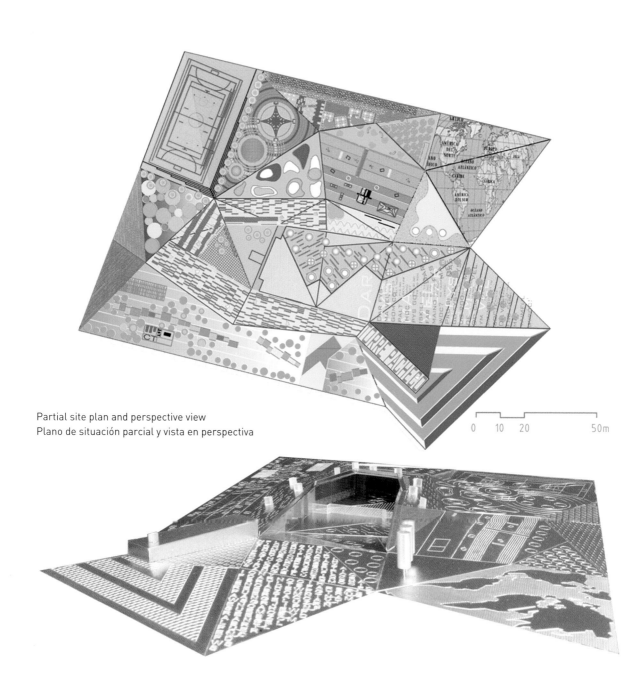

Partial site plan and perspective view
Plano de situación parcial y vista en perspectiva

0   10   20   50m

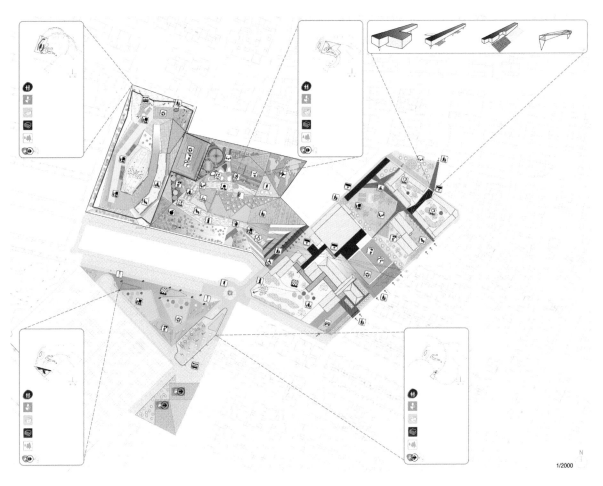

1/2000

Pictographic diagram of services
Diagrama pictográfico de los servicios

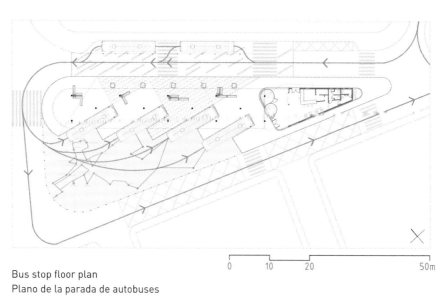

Bus stop floor plan
Plano de la parada de autobuses

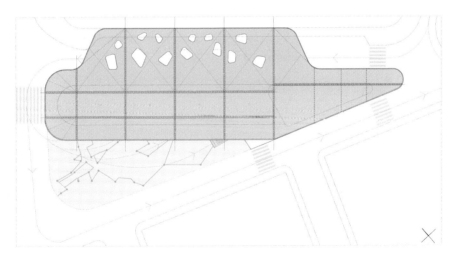

Bus stop roof plan
Plano de cubierta de la parada de autobuses

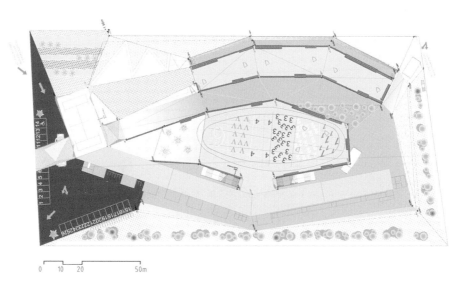

Partial site plan. Library
Plano de situación parcial. Biblioteca

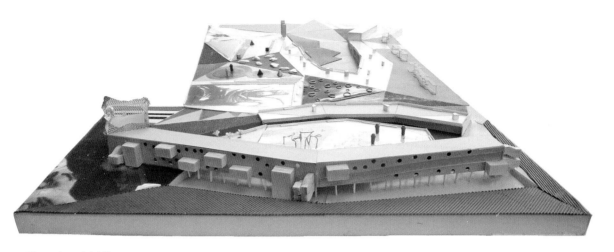

View of model. Library
Vista del modelo. Biblioteca

Rizhao Visitor Center

Rizhao, China

ARCHITECT:
HHD_FUN
www.hhdfun.com

DIMENSIONS:
N/A

PHOTOGRAPHERS:
© Zhenfei Wang, Chenggui Wang

COLLABORATORS AND OTHERS:
HHD & XinChao Design (LDI);
H & J International (civil engineer);
FUDA (façade consultant)

The visitor reception center is located in the northern part of the Shanhaitian Park, near to the beach. The building has two storeys and the design was created in order to minimize its impact and adapt it to the natural environment. The interior located in the subsoil holds shops, cinemas, restaurants, entertainment areas and public showers.

El centro de recepción de visitantes se sitúa en la parte norte del parque Shanhaitian, cercano a la playa. El edificio consta de dos plantas, y el diseño se creó para reducir al mínimo su impacto y hacer que se adaptara al entorno natural. El interior situado en el subsuelo alberga tiendas, cines, restaurantes, zonas de ocio y duchas públicas.

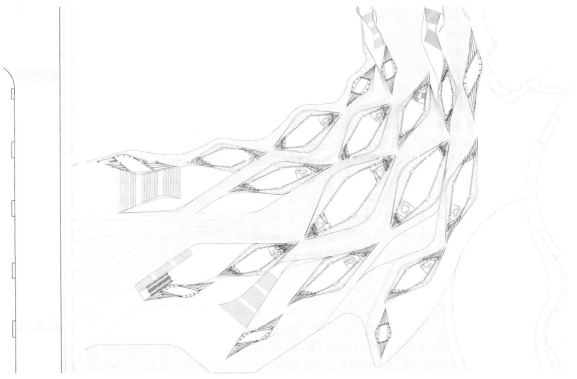

First floor plan
Planta primera

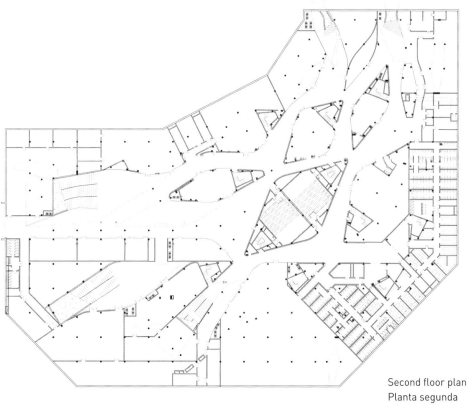

Second floor plan
Planta segunda

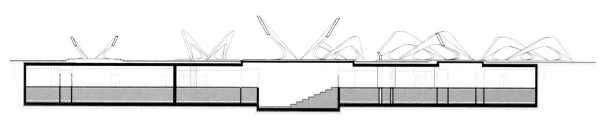

Section
Sección